The Sewing Room

The Sewing Room

Carla Funk

TURNSTONE PRESS

Turnstone Press
Artspace Building
018-100 Arthur Street
Winnipeg, MB
R3B 1H3 Canada
www.TurnstonePress.com

Turnstone Press gratefully acknowledges the assistance of the Canada Council for the Arts, the Manitoba Arts Council, the Government of Canada through the Book Publishing Industry Development Program, and the Government of Manitoba through the Department of Culture, Heritage and Tourism, Arts Branch, for our publishing activities.

 Canada Council for the Arts   Conseil des Arts du Canada   MANITOBA CONSEIL DES arts COUNCIL DU MANITOBA   Canada

Cover design: Doowah Design
Interior design: Sharon Caseburg
Printed and bound in Canada by Friesens for Turnstone Press.

Library and Archives Canada Cataloguing in Publication

Funk, Carla, 1974-
     The sewing room / by Carla Funk.

Poems.
ISBN-13: 978-0-88801-320-0
ISBN0-10: 0-88801-320-5

     I. Title.

PS8561.U8877S49 2006   C811'.54   C2006-905983-7

For my mother and my grandmothers.

Contents

The Banning of Beauty

Midnight in the Bedroom

The Sewing Room

Sunday School Lessons

Noah

Don't think of the flood.

Instead, pour the wine
and enter the tent where he lies
naked after the campfire
celebration and his old wife's dance
of thanksgiving as she lifted her hem,
swung in circles around high flames.

After months of sailing, he can still hear
the slosh of waves against the boat,
the night's gentle rocking.
Sleep swaddles the old man
in its massive hand. So much closer
to the truth: at the end as in the beginning
we are all laid naked before heaven.

For Noah, unwrapped and stretched out
in the night soaked with drink and love,
it is enough for the hard ground to hold him,
for the lowing of the sea-legged cattle,
for every living creature to be far-off
across the open plain.

For there to be dust instead of flood.

But for his son standing at the tent's entrance,
the ruined flesh holds before him a mirror.
The garden all over again, undressed
shame and a map to an unflinching future.

Like the boat hacked board by board
for the fire's fuel, his bones lay down
the message. There is no paradise
at the top of this mountain.
We're still watching the flames
slow-dance into ash.

Lot's Wife

Regret doesn't get any
clearer than this—
a wasp on the cheek
drilling through
what should have been
a jawbone, what
would have been
the place my husband
touched his thumb,
pressed his mouth
some dark nights ago.

Each morning the gazelles
lick grooves into my ankles
with their long black tongues.
My wrists thin a little every day.

The tiny bells and polished stones
that hung around my neck
have been stolen by ravens.
The threadbare bag I carried
spills open. A scrap of silver
hammered to a mirror
pulls down the sun
to flicker over me.

The ground blooms
and wanes its rock roses,
juniper, scattered violets.

Time is no looping
mountain trail on which
to double back. No,
it's an arrow shot from
a flaming city, a line of fire
that gets you from behind.

Knowing what I know now,
I would have held
that mirror in front of me
like a shield.

Leah

While Rachel wore the crown
of the Miss Mount Carmel pageant,
satin hair draped like a sash over her shoulders,
you, ever the runner-up, lay in your tent
with weak eyes and crooked teeth,
a book of lamentations written
across your veiled face.

Had you stood next to the one-eyed,
smash-nosed girl from the tribe next door,
or the fish-lipped peasant daughter
of your father's hired hand,
you would have shone
bright as a slick new calf.

Your mother always told you
ugly is as ugly does, quit your blubbering,
look how your sister Rachel walks
with a basket on her head and a clay jar in each hand,
graceful as a doe on her way to the well,
and why can't you stand up straight?

Every family tree needs you
to bend down and peer into the shining pool,
to tell us ugly is a relative word,
that misunderstood sister of beauty
and second cousin, once removed,
of loneliness. Every story needs you
to show us the high path into mountains,
and once there, the myrtle and wild olive
blooming in desolate clefts.

Down at the stream shaded by sycamores,
your face hangs over the water,
empty as an old bucket. Dreams
of a wedding tent sewn with desire,
gold and firelight seem to float away;
brittle leaves, broken twigs.

From the dirt at your feet,
you pick a fallen fig
and peel back the blighted skin.

The Burning Bush

Last day of school before summer vacation.
I'm fifteen and lying on my back at the cutbanks,
having bummed my first cigarette,
throat burning and red eyes blinking back stars.

The bikini girls splash waist-deep in the river
and recite obscene poems to the boys on shore
who flick bottle caps at them, and drag
on their smokes, drag on their smokes.

In the dry grass, I'm sweating off the gin
while the Pentecostal preacher's kid tells me
he's sick of his father's sermons, the same stories
over and over again, maybe it's about time

we make up new ones. Like maybe
instead of walking on water, Jesus freezes
the waves into a lake of ice, then
double-axels his way to the disciples

who hunker facedown in their wooden boat
frozen at the lake's centre. Or instead
of Moses and the burning bush,
it's a flaming camel God talks through.

And this boy goes on to wonder
if the camel carries a month's supply of water
in its hump, could it put out its own fire and
would it smell like one giant barbecue

out in that desert and couldn't you totally
go for a burger right now, take off
and fly out of this town on a winged chariot
with a souped-up v-8 engine?

Blurry-eyed at the river, I'm pinned under
the skywriter's blue, cirrus smoke
in ghost-hand overhead, a scrolled message
splitting me from my maker.

Instead of a burning bush, it's a preacher's drunk son
talking God. Instead of Egypt, a small town, low river
dividing who I am from who I am,
cutting the promised land in half.

Samson and Delilah

The Lucy and Ricky of the Old Testament, this act
would be all conniving Delilah and her hair-brained schemes,
Samson the superhero hit, his muscles a walking headline—
Sam slays thousands with the jawbone of an ass—
and their tabloid love all over the camp.

When Samson comes home from a sweaty day
at the winepress, Delilah's at the door
in her sleekest kitchen dress, hair tied up
in shiny knots and a sweet fig up her sleeve.
I've had a long day, she sighs, so do that thing
where you flex and twitch your pecs, give me
a shiver and a bolt of lightning inside.

Sucker for the skin, he strips down to nothing
and gives his wife a show until it's bedtime in their tent
and she's got him where she wants, the audience
sensing danger in the swollen soundtrack
when she hums tell me the story of all this strength,
her fingers in his hair, velvet lips against
his ear. Tell me the secret.

Imagine the laugh track this side of heaven
when Samson wakes to find his biceps
flaccid as an empty wineskin, a pair of
scissors and fistful of his hair in Delilah's hand
and all the neighbours gawking through the window
at his shorn weakness, man who once slew
hundreds, now slain by desire.

In the series finale when his hair has grown enough
to give back his strength, and he stands
in the backyard barbecue of the Philistines,
the camera zooms in to a shot of his hands
pressed against the temple columns, cuts to
his burnt-out eyes and pans heavenward.
This time, the gasp that goes up through the audience
is no pre-recorded cue. The tremor on the set
and the white dust falling has nothing to do with special effects,
nothing to do with the script's surprise end,
the sudden cancellation with no hope of reruns.

Daniel in the Lions' Den

We all have our dens. Our lions.

Thrown down into the stench
of piss and dung, we fumble
through gathered bones, squint at
old blood painted on walls
and try like the dream-weary prophet
to decipher those basement narratives
into happy endings.

But Lord, I want to read the story's
missing pages. I want to turn
the silence inside-out like a pocket
and shake free your secrets.

I want to choose the smoothest stone
and hurl it back at you. Hit the tender spot
and bring you down.

Make you step through the hidden doorway
and lay one gnarled hand upon the beast;
same hand that flung light, split the sea,
scooped up clay.

I want to draw you down to the floor
beside me and lean back against this wall,
let the words we say to each other
tone with the low thrum of purring
that echoes off stone. Two friends
talking through darkness, as though
in a house lit by torch-glow.

Into my empty cup, you pour
a swill of wine, deep drink
to pull me through the night.

What you offer, I swallow.

Epiphany

For some it comes like cresting
a hilltop on bicycle to find
the slow purple horizon,
a pleasant coast into consciousness.

For some it's a telegram that drops to the table
from the messenger's shaking hand.

Or it's the smoke alarm shrieking burnt toast
over the heart's morning colic.

For others it's a butcher chucking
a ham hock down onto brown paper
sudden and brutish as the stained apron
upon which he smears his hands.

And for the newlywed young woman
who steps into this butcher's shop
to purchase a tender cut for her man,
it grips the heart's most vital valve,
all those brilliant slabs of flesh
hung like lanterns above her head,
her wedding night a flash of heat
in the body's most delicate mechanisms.

In cartoons it's a light bulb burst above
the brain, the idea causing the fingers to snap
then a blur of rush lines as the character zooms
off screen while our cartoonist holds a dull pencil
above the empty page, waits for his own illumination.

A revelatory manifestation of a divine being
says the dictionary, thinking back to the camels
sulking over months' worth of desert, the Magi
who knelt at the foot of the boy Jesus,
their hands lifted to stroke the dark
head of God, a wound that infects
every blank gesture after.

I'll take mine any way I can get it,
anything for a flame in night's black tunnel,
anything for a feast in the winter's bleak light.

Angel of Stupidity

For the kid who licks the frozen
tetherball post in February;

for the boy who stares into the barrel of his gun
to see how far down the pellet rests;

for the great aunt who practises her pogo stick
on the high and rail-less deck, this angel comes—
bold-winged, brazen and dependable,
part lifeguard, part paramedic,
part SWAT team dispatcher.

For the bored youth who lines
the railroad tracks with dimes to see
whether stories of tragic train wrecks
come true, this angel bends down,
with its wing-tip flips off the coins.

For the girl who accepts a ride home
from the gravel pit party with a guy
whose pickup spins eternal gravel,
whose fingernails creased with grease
tap the dash in time to Megadeath,
whose best joke involves her the morning after,
this angel pulls the spark plug, punctures
the tire with a sharpened quill.

For the man who takes a run from the top of the cliff
in a homemade hang-glider, having skimmed
the instructions in a language he does not speak,
this angel tangles a length of rope around the foolish ankle.

For the woman who balances atop
a hundred-year-old ladder to prune her apple tree's
highest branch, this angel waits at the bottom,
wings spread out like a safety net, ready
to ease the timeless, predictable fall.

Pride

The guy in the shiny three-piece suit
strolls the sidewalk, swinging his briefcase.

With his free hand, he tosses an orange
into the air. At first, a few inches.
Then a foot high. Then two feet up.

Worked to the rhythm of his stride,
it's a game to play on this busy sidewalk
while traffic wheels by. The orange,
a tiny planet he throws into orbit,
then catches to draw the eyes
of cruising drivers, including mine.

When he steps over a ridge
of uneven cement and the tip
of one buffed shoe catches,
when his briefcase smacks concrete
and cracks open a chaos of paper,
his white shirt plants chest-down
on the sidewalk, when the orange rolls
off the curb and into the intersection
where cars and buses pull to a stop,
it's still a kind of game, but now a level
playing field, an honest set of rules—
gravity and the cosmos calling foul
beneath a red and blinking light.

As he lifts himself from the ground
and brushes off, his is a fate for which
I send up thanks, that rising heat of pleasure
in the chest, little hot air balloon
firing its burners toward the sky
far above this stumbling earth,
farther even than the stars.

Sloth

It's natural to think first of the animal
lazing in the rainforest.

How he claws leaves from branches
in slow motion whenever his stomach
remembers the word hunger.

How he hangs there a while wondering about . . .
whatever . . . as the rest of the day
unfolds like a tongue from within
a wide arboreal yawn.

How like us, he drags himself
across the earth, one slow toe
after the other, as if wading
through a slough of molasses
or despondency.

How like us, he dozes the days away
beneath the sun, that dangling gold watch
pulled from the sky's pocket . . .

how he finds ways to pass the time
or perhaps, let time pass him.

Wrath

In hell, dismemberment while alive
is the consequence for wrath,
which could explain why tonight
our bedroom feels a little like
a slaughterhouse. Your face
like a knife blade catching light.
This gash of silence.

Me biting my tongue, you
biting yours.

All the clichés—fire,
steam shooting from the ears,
the flared whites of the eyes—
seem so tame this evening.

What you've done, what we've said—
no matter how comic book our love quarrel—
boots objectivity out the door,
bolts the lock against common sense.

The invisible line I have drawn
down the length of the bed
only bolsters the argument, keeps me here,
you there, our backs to one another.

Don't let the sun go down on your anger
is the one piece of wisdom
my mother toasted on our wedding day,
lifting a wineglass to the chandelier.

I imagine somewhere,
in another time zone,
on a brighter and far-off continent,
the sun's hoisted high overhead,
a white flag burning.

Greed

George Pencz, a 16th century German artist, produced a series of engravings
in which he used animals to depict each of the seven deadly sins. For greed,
he chose the frog.

When the princess promised the frog
anything, anything if only he would
dive down into the well
and bring back her golden ball,
anything seemed like enough.

After years in a haze of bog-flies,
his mind grown soggy, he'd forgotten
what it felt like to want.
Her trinket boxes stuffed with jewels,
her heirloom crown, even
a seat at the royal table—
she'd offered it all.

So the frog leapt the dry mile to the castle
and pitched himself against the door
until the princess opened up.
He shared her steaming plate,
the wine in her silver cup,
edged his way onto her velvet lap,
took whatever she would give.

Next evening, he knocked
again at the palace door, begged
the princess to coax a croak
again and again from his waxy throat,
as if that would be enough.
What more, she asked,
what more on this earth
can you possibly want?

On the third night,
he breathed beside her
on the cotton pillowcase,
green suit of his skin stretched
taut, white vault of her body
cracked open under moonlight.
Everything in his cool blood
burned. He wanted,
he wanted more.

Envy

Once in hell,
the punishment for envy
involves submersion
in freezing water,

which I imagine,
in the middle of all those flames,
is a welcome change
from the fire, the brimstone,
the eternal burning.

While the envious chill,
everyone else looks on
and sweats, eyes shiny
as blown glass,
wanting that baptism
to be their own.

Lust

In Dante's *Inferno*, the lustful
spend eternity in hell's second circle,
sucked up in a blowing tornado,
the whirr of their earthly passions
manifested in a freakish force of nature,
a carnival ride that never ends.

Imagine their surprise when they arrive
on the outskirts of town and see
how long the lineup is, how
everyone who waits here stands
naked and shifting, a little nervous
on this sweltering stubbled field.

It's a view they've spent years craving,
but now the heat's too hot. The flesh
slides off, pools around the ankles
like fallen trousers, and their bones
melt like ice cream at a summer fair.

As they shuffle forward to board
the attraction, the screams they hear
could be girls on a roller coaster's drop,
could almost, if they close their eyes,
sound like pleasure.

Gluttony

Like the fat kid on race day, Gluttony
is the last one on the track, well behind
Lust, Greed, Anger and the others
who have already been handed their ribbons.

While Pride, with his champion's trophy
and shiny tracksuit, stands on the wobbly platform
and waves to the cheering crowds,

Gluttony's still chugging
toward the finish, face bright
as a chokecherry tart,
heart like a pound cake
swelling in his chest.

Eat, drink and be merry,
the spectators whoop,
as if there's no great harm in indulgence,
as if nobody sees Gluttony as a real contender.

Sure, maybe he'll never
be a real threat,
but no one can say he's not trying.

Vespers

At the window, day kneels
down to evening, and God
tugs at the shirtsleeve.

The dark ghost-shape of a deer
cruises by on the other side
of the glass, and I press my hand
to the pane as though I'm some
modern rendering of Eve
before the garden's
brokenness fell in.

There is grace enough
to hold me here, bring the night
on like a cold compress
to the forehead
hot with memory's burning.

The rain picks up, unfolds
green shadows into spring.
Always, God slips in at the flaw,
infects everything.

The Sewing Room

Flashlight Tag

In the time before lovers, before the urgent pulse
and the doorway's loaded glance, before night
opened a room with candles burning low
and a pair of hands to untie the darkness,

in the time of green and summer evenings
after supper to the rhythm of lawn sprinklers
and bicycle tires left spinning in the gravel driveway
to the tune of *one potato two potato three potato four*
children scatter to the trees, the woodshed, the barn;

the one with the flashlight presses his face
into his hands and counts to fifty, calls *ready-*
or-not-here-I-come for the hunt, small bodies
curled into the rims of logging truck tires
or flattened beneath back porches
so even their shadows melt into the ground.

To be the one who seeks means solitude
and the silence of your shoes on the damp grass.
The dull beam's concentric gold rings cast
over the picnic table, birdhouse, snapdragon bed
a rippled lake of fear. And you feel
in those first few moments alone in the world,
explorer in a land of darkness or the last person
alive at earth's end, your heart grabbed
by panic's black glove

                    until a laugh flickers
in the underbrush, a hand dips down from a tree
and you sweep the landscape with light, catch
a flash of pant leg, the fluorescent stripe of a running shoe
and relief comes on hard, you're not the only child
here, you're not the only one caught
and swallowed by night, not the last
person walking this planet.

Incendiary

Flashback to age three-and-a-half.
I'm crouched in the sand beneath
the clothesline stand, my mother above
hanging out the day's washing.

I lean forward, mouth open as if waiting
for a doctor's swab. A floating hand
holds a lighter to my tongue,
that incendiary trigger.

A simple explanation for the leaning
I do later, over the bathroom sink
as my mother scrubs with a bar of Ivory
the cussing off my tongue.

But soap and water don't snuff out
this kind of flame. Words
still rise heated to the surface,
spit out their starry cinders.

In the forest of life, the tongue is
the arsonist's best weapon,
a jerry can sloshing with gas,
a box of strike-anywhere matches.

No wonder my words fly out
like sparks and make you pull away
anxious of the burn, leery
of this overflowing fuel.

Secrets

Every family has at least one.

For us, it was the ice cream
Dad scavenged from the town dump,
half-melted cartons chucked by the local dairy
when their freezers went on the fritz.

We stood over the slick rainbow of boxes
he stacked in our basement deep freeze,
an underground ice cream parlour opened
inside the bare concrete room,
a flavour for every day in July.

Don't tell, Dad said. Not anyone.

That summer, blackflies swarmed
the nights as always. Dad blazed
the wild acre for a new garden,
our tomcat went missing for a week
and came back with half his right ear.
Mum fell off a ladder washing windows,
broke both her wrists. These stories
we spoke freely over the building of tree forts,
backyard games of scrub and kick-the-can.

Hot days, we'd crank the lawn sprinkler high
and run with neighbourhood kids
through the flying swathe of rain.
Mum would haul the ice cream
from the dark basement, one carton at a time,
and spread them out on the picnic table
for us to choose. My brother and I shared looks
across our friends, kept our mouths shut,
while Mum, in slow motion,
scooped our dripping cones,
the white casts of her hands
holding out the secret
for everyone to taste.

Dreamspeak

At the bottom of the blackwater lake
a girl in an invisible two-piece
sits, knees pulled to her chest,
hands around her ankles. She's anchored
to this spot, lungs in a chokehold.

A cutthroat angles by, cigarette butt
sagging from his lips. In his tail,
a rusted hook. He circles her,
inside fin dragging across her
back, along her forearm.

Why do you play so hard-to-get?
His words come in bubbles,
dreamspeak that's clear enough
to hear even through the murk.

When his cloudy eye levels
against her own, it's a look
that double-dares, shoots
the gaze of every man her way.

Dragonflies skim the lake surface,
iridescent lures. The bodies on shore
oil and burn. Overhead,
the sun aims its searchlight.

Word Association

Backyard
My father's stained blue jeans.

Cigarette smoke kite-tailing into grey.

The chopping block he leans over.

A stretched white neck
and the axe sinking down.

Fine red mist on his dark hands,
on the silver blade.

Sound of wing-flutter
like a book of endless pages
turning toward its end.

Party
Bonfire orange at the gravel pit.

Pickup tailgate stacked with beer.

Cranked-up bass that beats
the chest, sub-woofers, tweeters,
Metallica thrum on high.

Baseball caps with curved bills
everywhere. Girls in acid-wash
who hold their hands
open to the flames.

Downtown
Sidewalk concrete split by cold.

Late winter scraped over the road's
centre line, a meridian of mud
and snow and oil.

One post office, glass doors
taped with announcements
of the latest dead.

Fourteen gas pumps,
three grocery stores,
one curling rink,
one high school.

One traffic light,
and everywhere,
pickup trucks.

River
Inner tubes in July, floating
from the new bridge to the old,
hot black rubber burning
our backs red.

Some kid jumping
every summer off the top
of the wooden bridge.

Make-out dates at the cutbanks,
soft welts in the shore grass
where bodies have lain.

Every August,
one drowning.

Down into Our Potato Patch

Tires plowing slow motion through
the black dirt, Grandpa's maroon
Oldsmobile rolls and my dad stands
dumb-footed in the driveway, looks
from the car to his father beside him,
unsure of who should move first,
whether jumping at the steering wheel
would be worse than letting it all happen
as it's happening now, dark green
plants bent in the bumper's wake,
small hills torn down and scattered
purple blooms. This landscape a scaled-down
version of natural disaster, an aerial
photograph of some leafy other world
after a hurricane's swathe.

Neither man moves.

Grandpa flicks his home-rolled cigarette
into a puddle, eyes holding fast to his long car.

The tires sink to a stop
at the potato patch's edge.

My dad unsnaps a shirt pocket and
pulls out an Export A, cups his hand
to grab the lighter's spark in the evening breeze.

Nothing is said. As if there is nothing wrong
with this picture, there is no garden
cut through with ruin, there is no car.
No words to fill the decades between these men,
no forgiveness, no atonement.

When my dad breathes out
a long sigh, there is no smoke.

When Grandpa shoves
his hands into his coat pockets
the keys that rest there
make no sound.

Hawaii

The photograph most remembered is
not the pineapple field, the sugar cane plantation,
canoe show dolphins dancing backward through waves,
is not aquarium penguins torpedoing down plastic slides,
ukulele women swishing their grass skirts,
not the luau pig rising from hot sand.

The photograph most remembered
is always the one not taken, that memory left
floating in the cerebrum's temporal lobe.

Back at the beach, my father in his pin-striped trunks
sat on the edge of his lawn chair
working his cigarette to a glow
under the palm's lazy sway.

On the pool's edge, my mother dipped her legs,
embarrassed in her ruffle-skirted bathing suit,
polka-dotted and sticking out like a fat thumb.

From ocean to sand pile, my brother and I
packed pails, building some imaginary world.

My father's shout from the pool deck
brought us running to where he stood
pointing into the water, my mother
in a starfish float at the deep end.
Facedown and sinking, until
a lifeguard dove from his chair,
peeled her off the bottom, her body
sagging over his shoulder.

Hotel security and a crowd of tourists
rushed in to watch the lifeguard
tip back my mother's head,
place his mouth over hers
while my father stood over them,
cigarette still burning.

When the paramedics in their white shirts
and tans arrived with a stretcher,
she had already sputtered awake,
lay wrapped in a blanket on a chaise lounge,
wet hair dripping in her eyes.

Later, in the hotel room, when she asked again
how did it happen, who saved her,
my father said he saw the whole thing,
that if it hadn't been for him
she would never have survived.
She'd be forgotten, still floating
in the deep end, waiting
for someone to rescue her.

Tijuana

Like that game where you spin the globe
and with eyes closed plant your finger
on a surprise continent to see where
you really belong—Sweden, the Ivory Coast,
an almost invisible Fijian island—
we stepped off the tour bus disoriented.

A blind woman stood on the sidewalk
with her burro and held out her hand
until Dad threw a quarter.

In shop windows, milky-eyed posters
of Michael Jackson hung in the sunlight
yellowing beside figurines of bullfighters
and the Blessed Virgin Mary.

A boy rolled by on his homemade skateboard,
no legs and just a baggy t-shirt pinned
up to his chest, his fists pumping
the concrete for speed.

At the end of the day, the bus driver
snapped a photograph of our family—
my father in his newly bartered
leather jacket leaning against
a cinder block wall, his wide new hat
bashing my mother in the forehead,
my brother holding up a Chinese star,
me beside him with a fistful of paper flowers.

We flew home that night with sombreros
on our laps, blue velvet trimmed with gold
and sequins sewn to the cap and brim
in rainbows of firework explosions.

As the airplane's landing gear pulsed down
into our small valley of snow, patchwork
of farm and forest, my head flashed
with bright dresses and bare feet,
that half-boy wheeling by on the sidewalk,
a globe spinning backwards and off-kilter
in the compass of a new geography.

Continental Drift

A glass vase of flowers glows on the sill.
Your mother's hands down
the collar of your shirt

while my own mother weeds
the strawberry patch, and hollers
to me across the garden
for another shovel and bucket.

Music owns your mornings, your father
bent over the piano, pushing sound
around the room like furniture. A hollow
oak chair in the shape of a c minor scale.
The long fermata hanging there
like a frame without its photograph.

My mornings owned too by music
of a different key, my father tuning in
the local country and western station,
hitting his hand on the kitchen table
in a limping two-step.

—

You learn to smoke cigarettes
at your uncles' knees, with laughter and coarse jokes
in the living room after dinner.

Already at fourteen you are more man than boy
having lain the night through with a girl,
having known to push back her hair and speak
the kind of soft promises she will write down
in her journal and read years later
when she grows lonely for yesterday.

Though she will think of calling you
on certain nights, you will move on,
passenger on a train that doesn't even stop
for beauty fastened to the tracks.

On another continent, I grow into a version
of this girl, impatient for romance,
more child than woman. Constantly
I am lying down for the oncoming
wreck, bracing myself for impact.

—

In one room, you play Debussy,
piano pouring waterfalls of light
through the house

while I stand in the slaughterhouse
with the bristled scrape of my father's knife
over the pig's steaming belly.

Your Copenhagen, a city of goddess
and mermaid, windmills and fountains,
the Queen flying her colours over the palace.

My Copenhagen a pinch of snuff
tucked in my father's lower lip.
A long afternoon of dark juice
spat into the butchering yard.

—

Across an ocean and a continent
and countries in between, movements
of history play themselves out
to bring us into the same room.

Outside your window, people in dark coats
move over frozen sidewalks. Winter hangs
a black and white photograph.

Inside my faraway room,
locked in by February's ice,
my hands over the piano keys
play a different set of notes,
variations on a countering theme.

The Sewing Room

Tonight it's the scissors' cool, silver
sound slicing through a bolt of fabric
that takes me home to her, sends me barefoot
to the bottom of the stairs and into the sewing
room where she sits with her back to the dryer
tumbling its load of clothes.

Though evenings are full of projects—a patchwork
blanket of scraps from rummage sale castoffs,
mending of my brother's school pants or
my father's torn cuffs, tonight
I see she is sewing for me, a Christmas dress—
the flowered one with the blue velvet bodice
and soft laces that tie at the waist.

Later I will stand on the padded brown chair
as she kneels on linoleum to tack
the hem in place. She will pull each pin
from between her lips, the points
snagging my knees as I turn a slow-motion circle
while she checks the evenness of her work.

Upstairs, the mantel clock winds down
its song. As evening crosses over into bedtime,
the house quiets and the rest of us
tuck in for the night. Down the hall, my brother
is reading another book about rocketry
and undiscovered galaxies.
My father lies asleep on the living room floor,
land of TV shadows on mute.

Downstairs, my mother stays at her sewing,
bends over her machine while the needle works
up and down the seams to bind together
the pattern's many separate parts.

Some nights it's as if she's driving us to another place.
With her right foot pressing the pedal
and with the tiny engine's even hum,
our house seems to move through the dark subdivision,
past town limits, traveling down a highway line
that stitches asphalt to horizon
in another mending together of the elements.

The Blue Spruce Cafe

Unlike the other fathers in town
who can show off a son's new logging truck
or a daughter's 12-point buck
shot down in a clearing off Bear Head Road,
my dad comes and goes empty-handed
to the morning coffee shop.

What's he supposed to do
with a poet for a daughter?
What to bring to this Formica table
of burning cigarettes and toast plated
by a waitress named Dot?

Is it too much to imagine him
pulling a book from his back pocket,
cracking open the spine as he holds up a hand
to say shut up, fellas, listen to this,
then begin to read a poem—
maybe the one about him shooting the cocker spaniel
after she caught her hind leg in a fox trap.
The kind of poem that would make the men
shake their heads at the last line,
stare into the bottoms of their coffee cups
and hang a thought in the silence,
a sort of uneasy applause
for that feeling that rises in them.

Maybe it would catch, poetry
at The Blue Spruce Cafe, poetry
at the truck stop, poetry read aloud
over the local country and western station
in between ballads by Tanya Tucker
and The Oak Ridge Boys.

Soon the men would write their own poems,
pulling from their down-filled vests
scraps of inked-up paper, haiku
about icy roads, a burned-out bush camp,
the head cook who hanged himself
during February's cold snap.

They would see things about themselves
they never had before,
their smoky breakfast tables quieter,
no holding court over the radio's headlines.
Their mugs cooling. The steam of coffee.
Sound of liquid poured from the pot.
All of them holding up their cups
thirsty for the bottomless drink.

Reconstruct

Sometimes he is building things in my mind,
my childhood a scattered town
of sandboxes, picnic tables, woodsheds.

Armed with brown paper bags full of nails,
a level, a hammer, his handsaw,
he makes Saturdays a blueprint.

In stained coveralls, he kneels
twelve feet above ground
on the tree fort floor,
measures joists and angles,
his wide, flat pencil grooving
over two-by-fours.

It is not evening with its stumbling
and shadows. Not the heavy head
of morning that hangs
over the breakfast plate.

It is afternoon.
Sun pries between cracks
and through knotholes.
My father shifts his cigarette
to the corner of his mouth
and swings the hammer down.

This is a moment I can hang on to,
something worth inhabiting.

When he unrolls the rope ladder
from the freshly cut window,
I am waiting at the bottom,
ready to climb up.

The Banning of Beauty

The Banning of Beauty

Lock the gates against splendour,
black out every luxury and pleasure—
tear from the country's lexicon the word *lovely*.

Call beauty an infection,
and it only spreads,
roots deeper in the earth.

In the uniform streets, people on bicycles
pedal out whole dynasties of verse,
each downward foot a poem's stressed syllable
pumping forward through silence.

In the oil and steam of the factories,
workers compose love songs for bells and drums,
make of the mind a rebel orchestra pit.

No silk threads embroidering their slippers
with phoenix, lotus, a dragon's fire, the women
find other ways to shine. Behind the drawn curtains
of their shadowed houses, they hang
polished teaspoons from the ceiling,
catch what light they can
from the candles' glow.

Children, knowing the laws by which they are governed,
hide marbles under loose floorboards,
cover the glass bowls of goldfish with dark cloth
and slide them under the beds.
While they sleep, scales flicker beneath,
stowaway cells of a dreamworld waiting
to be woken and entered.

Under the muted palette of night,
across the grey city and in another room,
a man's hand traces the body of his beloved,
his finger a brush that paints her skin
with the calligraphy of bamboo and plum,
all the flesh alive, a hundred flowers blooming.

Winter Night: Voyeur

Across the road, the neighbour slams his shovel
into the layer of ice that cakes his driveway, the blade
breaking the crust into small continents,
the pavement a shattered map he hoists
to a pile on the snow-covered lawn.

Whatever sets him on late shift in night's anxious field
fuels the work; his body is a crude machine of shadow,
shoulder bent to the frozen ground.
                                        His breath hangs
pockets of fog against the garage light's glow.
They rise, then vanish, small weather
in this fissure of darkness.
                                        He takes off a glove
to wipe his forehead and lean on his shovel, to lift
his face to the sky's open quarry. He stands,
a question raised on this finite range.

The moon shakes out its fool's gold,
little stars. Out of the cave of dreaming,
we drag our tools and set to work, splitting
the earth in pieces, dredging the glory hole.

Afterlife Telegrams

When the messengers arrive, light as gauze
and glowing, there's already a lineup forming
on shore, souls pushing forward to hear
what's been happening in their absence.

It's mail call in the hereafter
as the ghostly couriers seek out their addressees,
a hollering of names across the diaphanous crowds,
everyone eager for news.

Some messengers bring tidings of joy—
    Gladys and Edward finally tied the knot.
Some speak reassurance—
    The kids are fine, living it up at the farm.
Others deliver overdue apologies, each word
a small polished stone of remorse—
    He wasn't worth it.
    I'm sorry about the monkey.
    You were right. I should have let you drive.

But just as in life there's always someone forgotten,
at least one empty-handed and standing alone,
no telegram for her, no message at all.
Like the bride left behind and waiting
to hear word from the front lines,
she wonders how her beloved's making out
in the battle, wonders if he still carries
her memory like a picture in his left shirt pocket.

While the others float away trading
news, each heart rising
like a child's balloon into the ether,
she lingers on the edge of that silver river
and shades her eyes toward
the horizon's narrowing trench.
Thinks, if there were such a thing
as tomorrow, maybe then
the waiting wouldn't seem so long.

Permission

Book spine folded open
casual as a man in summer repose,
the poet speaks from his place on the shelf.

Why is it so hard for you to see
things as they are, he breathes.
Go ahead and praise the plum tree,
laud the spleen, look out the cracked window
and see the neighbour's cows
fastened to the fields by their ever-chewing
mouths. Really they are not cows,
the poet tells me, but sage nomads
of the pastoral realm, calm
hostages of melancholy.
And evening sky is a dark plate
over which salt has been shaken,
a panther's hide stretched
over the scaffolding of night,
anything you want it to be.

Easy for him to say.

Outside my window, a grey thunderhead
leans over the trees, winded amnesiac.
Rain taps out a message I struggle to decode.

But now the poet is climbing from his book,
shaking off sand from some South American beach.
The sea drips from his hair. A purple starfish
tattoos itself above his heart.

When he comes near, I hold out
my hand, my open palm
pale as a slip of paper, the lines there
waiting to be signed.

If

The word *if* is a hinge
that swings between the real
and the not, opens the door
to a room without walls,
a room part forest, part air,
part darkness and a hand
sliding up the bedcovers,
two parts shiver, one part desire.

The word *if* is a continent
of invention, where the six-legged,
swamp-eyed creatures you drew
as a child graze in purple fields,
the mist hanging low
over their many-horned heads.
On this skiff of earth, you
are the first inhabitant, the one
to name and have dominion over
the flora and fauna of your hands,
the one to call it good.

The word *if* hides behind the temporal lobe,
between cerebellum and medulla oblongata.
The brain's hidden weapon, it's what causes
a girl from some interior town
to become an astronaut, Da Vinci
to dream glorious machines
that hover over earth, a flea to join
the circus. Were this part
of the brain any larger, believe
scientists, people would fly.

The word *if* is an insect
that lives underground,
with the snout of a pig,
the skink's reptilian tail,
the caterpillar's many legs.
Though nocturnal, the *if*
emerges in spring from its
winter hibernation, grows a sudden
pair of wings and buzzes off
through the zigzag sky.

If only, say the zoologists,
we could track its migratory
paths, we might find the
resting ground, graveyard
for all the dying ifs, the place
where it plummets from sky
and sinks into earth,
as if it never existed,
as if it were
pure imagination.

Dream History of the Telephone

Because of the cartographer's desire
and the long lines of maps,
                              because of rivers
that rise every spring to flood
roads, stop travel,
                              because of the silence
of ink and the letter's refusal
to speak aloud,
                              because his sweet wife
Mabel left on the train for a long visit
with her sister,
                              Alexander Graham Bell began
to dream.
                    After an evening at the circus,
he dreamed a globe strung with
a glitter of tightropes, and a million
dark-haired versions of his wife toeing
along the balance.
                              The next night, a dream
of spiders, their webs elongated in silk
bridges over the town's lake, Mabel's fingers
in the runnel of his spine.
                                        And finally,
in the third evening's sleep, a vision
of his own open body, slick pathways of veins
carrying the blood's lonely messages
in microscopic envelopes, cells and nerves
moving at the speed of sound.

He writes on the yellow page of his notebook:
February 14
Mabel away two weeks now, the kitchen empty
and our bed cold.
                    Dragged the parlor-organ
into the back room in hopes of sending Mr. Watson
a clear song.
            So far the world is quiet.

He goes to sleep with the sound of his wife's
soft humming pressed into his head, and dreams
her perfect ear laid against his chest.

                                    February 28
The trains stopped and still no Mabel.
Today I stood in the closet a full thirty minutes
for her smell, pale lilacs and vanilla
in the wool sweaters she left hanging.

Nothing but crackling noise over the wires;
still, Mr. Watson hopeful.

For nights he dreams a telegram with skin, lips
almost close enough to kiss, and wakes
to the mournful rumble of engines over rails.

March 8
At the sound of tomorrow's first train
I will pretend to set out to meet her.

Today, set steel-spring close to but not quite
touching the electro-magnet's core.

In the next room Mr. Watson
swears he hears
a pure musical note.

Already I see her shadow
in the lamplight,
the smooth curve of her hip
upon waking.

That evening he sleeps with
the window open, a blade of moonlight
across the bedcovers, night
eerie in its calm and his dream
a moving picture of deafness. His wife
throat-deep in a black pool, her splashes
and useless flailings, his back turned
away from water's edge.

March 9
This morning, the early train's
shrill whistle and a cold cup of tea
with Mr. Watson.

Again, I dream her mouth
to my ear, sound of her breathing
like a current through my bones.

Metaphor

Let us begin with a blanket of snow,
though we both know there is no blanket,
no flannel down comforter sewn
of snowflakes, winter's invisible thread
stitched with needles of ice.

But what we do have is snow,
soft white spread over the ground,
the whole earth a bed that coaxes you to
crawl in, fall asleep.

Or, an ocean of snow, drifts piled up
in silver waves, everlasting sea
we sail in our sleigh, the surf
tossing froth in our faces.

So many possibilities in this place.
A canvas of snow, and you the artist
whose bootprints shadow
a rough sketch of winter.

Dancefloor of snow, making you the principal
in this season's choreography.

Table of snow, meaning the feast
of winter is upon us, the earth
gives up its bounty, and you
the guest of honour, crowned.

Like an explorer, a good metaphor sets out
holding one half of the torn map,
and comes back treasure-laden;
shows you with trembling hands
two things at once, real and imagined,
the shard of mirror
and the chest of gold bullion.

But the bad metaphor wanders
out like an explorer with vertigo,
heart full of awkward music,
head full of calculus, and hands
loaded with casino tokens.
He ends up in the nearest strip mall,
uncertain where to spend his money,
stumbles the sidewalks in search
of a payphone, a voice
to give direction.

Take this explorer home.
Sit him down and shake out his pockets.
Let him keep one thing only, perhaps his compass
so that the needle points north
toward a landscape of snow, back to
that white horizon holding out hope,
an invitation, and what could be
smoke over a graveyard, what
could be a field of winter crocuses,
what could be.

Muse

Mine is no uncorked chalice that spills out
a goddess of chiffon and ether, song-voiced
and floating above the ordinary
toward the canon of brilliant ideas.

Today, she's a far-off friend from high school
who calls to say she's going back
for more liposuction, this time
on belly, thighs and buttocks.

The first round didn't take, she says,
the bruising severe and for two weeks
she had to use a walker to get around the house,
the stapled line across her abdomen stretched taut
and muscles learning their new shape.

Only now, a year later, has the swelling begun to settle
and the red slashes of scar tissue fade,
but she's committed to this bodily arts and crafts pursuit
like a sculptor to her shapeless clay, bent
on stripping away flaws, a physical revision
that brings me back to the page
again, and all these words.

On a sterile white table is where I want to
lay down my poem, let the surgeon hold his wand
to the pale sheet, vacuum every loose adjective
and sagging phrase, slice from lazy metaphors
the flab, all the fat from language.

What sleeps beneath this makeshift glut,
what's wrapped beneath gauze and veil
is what I want most, and that voice
in my ear whispering, wake up.

Night Walk

Sky's black gloss and the street
a long mirror of sidewalk lights.

The wind pushes wet leaves and an empty
garbage bag slick with rain behind you;

your dark neighbourhood shakes
the folded map inside.

What makes the body pace
the night to sudden nowhere,

the feet wear down the earth's hard edges.
So the idea begins its slow erosion from stone.

Like the artist with his prophet hands
sculpting slabs of marble sliver-thin,

a father's hand on his small girl's forehead
soothing the fever toward sleep

or a man's naked back sanding down
the wood's rough cut, bone-smooth.

The blood with its desert silt pours on
in the anxious cities,

in you who walk the darkness
with that hand upon your shoulder

to wear away the heaviness,
to usher down the flesh.

Excess

You wake each day feeling the alphabet has grown
overnight, your mouth too full of words.

Even silence is a long vowel that will not end,
a five-mile tunnel of ricochet and echo.

You offer simple semaphores to pare things down;
your head in your hands instead of grief's explanation.

When you need help ordering the day's steps,
you cut memory down to a stone you can swallow.

Clear away the tables and chairs, clutter of dishes
and books, the ringing telephone and the clock's tick

until all that's left is one small room
the size of a grown man's skull.

With a key carved from bone, you unlock the door
and bend low to enter; strike a match to find

a place you call relief: that green and simple valley,
the sky unhinging its white ramp of clouds.

Allusion

In a lecture on allusion, the back row girl
asks about that writing on the wall,
all those purple mouths and goblets
gathered at the royal table when the hand ghosts
an indecipherable *mene mene tekel parsin*
but I'm no sorcerer for this King of Medes,
no translator of the divine in room A229.

Still, here I am at the chalkboard
with dust on my fingers, my crooked scrawl trying
to explain the history of God and prophets.
It's a Sunday school lesson gone haywire
as I rattle off Ezekiel's bones in the dry valley,
Hosea's prostitute wife a version of the Israelites'
unfaithfulness, but we're not onto metaphor yet.

I stand outside myself to hear this naïve tongue
say God like "John" or "Aunt Mary,"
and First Chronicles chapter three
as if it's a phone number, as if
Jesus is the neighbour next door
who lends me a cup of brown sugar
or a pinch of sage when the pantry lies bare.
As if I sit with him over tea and talk
lazy afternoons away, his beat-up sandals
traded for knitted slippers, his blue and white
robes replaced by sweatpants and t-shirt.

But we're on to Eliot's Magi now, three trees
on the low sky that hoist crosses in this room.
One boy's head lifts when the old white horse
gallops into the meadow of understanding.
A girl's mouth drops when the six dicing hands
hold out silver like a key to a locked door,
and the whole room bends down to read again,
quiet and listening for the other story,
the allusion this silence makes
to something outside ourselves.

Found

So often the story is not what we think.

On a morning walk, the earth in fragments
reveals an archaeologist's junkpile heart.

On a one-mile stretch of highway:
- a spoon holding the sun in its silver oval
- a smashed beer bottle
- a half-smoked cigarette
- a man's white shoe.

The asphalt reads like a rebus text,
simple objects tossed out to tell
something more complicated.

The roadside party in brown glass shards
reveals the whole bottle, the beer, the throat
that swallows, music that plays in the heads
of bored teenagers while they cruise
through the tunnel of adolescence.

The spoon that holds the shining sun
lies parallel to the blacktop as though set there
for an invited dinner guest.
This is the meal, the preparation,
the hope in the hands of a woman
unpacking boxes after a long move south
across prairie roads and mountains.
This is the mouth that held the silver spoon
which now feeds light to an open sky.

The half-smoked cigarette still smoulders
with the guy who wants to quit,
around the cluttered table at which he sits
each night, empty ashtray, flint and threat
of forest fire, his hesitancy around
each curve of highway and slope of road
as the police cruisers clock his speed.

The one white sneaker
that flies out the open window,
comes back to haunt a man's naked foot.
He stands in a parking lot, one shoe off,
one shoe on, looking through his trunk,
the backseat, rummaging through darkness,
that missing shoe nowhere and somewhere.
He wonders, what can a man do
with half a pair?

Taking Back the Garden

Let me begin by saying that my husband
is out of town on business, that night has a way of
coercing fear out of even the bravest, that
the moon is only a thin slice of orange
hanging in the sky's dark grove.

Let me add that thirty years ago,
this cottage was a chicken barn
in whose loft the farmer died, suddenly
and without warning—poison,
heart attack, dysentery—no explanation
ever satisfied his gumboot of a wife.

It's an eeriness I sit with now in this living room,
television on mute and the floorboards alert.
This creaking wood and shifting frame
seem to wake up with the evening,
trees remembering their forest roots, nocturnal
and talkative, but quiet enough for me to hear
the mouse that pads down the hall
and onto the linoleum.

From where I sit on the couch
with my feet tucked up,
he appears larger and more sinister
than those in picture books and cartoons.

In the dim green of the microwave's glowing clock,
the silhouette of whiskers over the cupboard doors
has the appearance of many thin blades.
His tail prongs the air like a pitchfork's sharpest tine.

When he shifts toward the stove and scratches
his way up the hanging towels onto the counter,
over to the fruit bowl and onto the softening pears,
the gorging begins. He digs his pointed
face into the flesh and begins to chew,
the small, wet sound of his feasting magnified
by the emptiness of the kitchen.

This is how the word *infestation* begins.
News of life beyond the trash can and the soggy field
travels along baseboards and into walls
to prove the exterminator's philosophy:
where there is one mouse, there soon will be many.

Stories of mice birthing blind, hairless litters in the insulation
are not ones I want to remember at this moment,
nor statistics of rapid breeding habits,
ability to squeeze through a knothole the size of a dime,
fondness for human hair as nesting material.

And I don't need history to crack open its chronicles
of soldiers eaten alive by swarms of mice
that descended like locusts into a sleeping valley of tents.
Don't want to hear about diseases these rodents spread
by nibble and scat, of their cannibalistic nature.

I'd rather stay awake to plan my methods of attack,
the traps I'll bait with cheese and peanut butter.
Stay right here on the sofa, wrapped in a tight, thick quilt
with the consolation of God who in the beginning
granted man dominion over every living thing
that moveth upon earth, even this mouse
eating his way through my fruit bowl, this creature
taking back the garden, bite by tiny bite.

Midnight in the Bedroom

Displacement

Take that last night in Rome.

The alley's streaks of light
brushed gold into the air.
Music from a café sang *stay, stay,*
stay another month amores,
notes that tugged our coat sleeves,
slowed our walk to a stroll
and then a stop below a balcony
lined with tomato plants,
their red more seductive
than any we could grow back home.

You looked at me as if my hair were black
instead of blonde, as if I sang instead of spoke.
When I rolled the language off my tongue
you bent to kiss a different pair of lips
than the one you know from home.
That alone was enough
to make me want to stay.

Let the fingerprints you left on my skin
in that country, that city, that villa
floating with dim light and distant voices
in the universe—let these fingerprints
stand for the syllables of a new language,
words we're learning all over.

Let the displacement of love into a strange land
stamp the body's passport with palmarosa
and sweet orange, cinnamon and frangipani,
scents we carry home when this journey ends.

Absence

Again, I fly off for a week of business
and the routine of our distance opens up

loneliness like a new row of seats.
Another lineup of guests files in to fill them.

When I try to block their entry, I end up
an unarmed stewardess, safety signs off-

kilter and full of mixed messages.
Dreams call forward all the standbys—

the grocery guy who offers free
pineapple samples at his wooden stand,

a highway roadman who tips the brim of his hat,
raises one eyebrow to my gaze,

the high school history teacher with his stiff tie
and broken handfuls of chalk, notes on the board

listing dangers of cross-continental journeys.
Mornings, my king-sized bed is traveled chaos.

Each night away I stand at the window,
air conditioner ghosting the curtains

as I say into the telephone, I mean it,
this hotel room is lonely without you.

Back at home, you're lying on the sofa
with a television flashing random faces;

outside my window, the cityscape flickers
on and off, signal fires on the horizon.

When you meet me at arrivals
with your hands hanging down, I want

to believe what they say about absence,
want to curb the wandering and trace

whatever's lost by time and miles;
love riding out the carousel darkness

and into the terminal light
where we stand, waiting to lay claim.

Bundling

If I could climb back inside the Kansas landscape,
back into a buggy drawn by two horses
into a village of plain dresses and starched white bonnets,
dark trousers and wide-brimmed hats—
if I could climb back inside the life of a young Amish
girl, I would spend the night with you
in my ancestors' attic bedroom.

Into long bundling sacks we'd slide,
a strong seam stitched between our bodies,
our faces flushed in lamplight.
We'd lie on a mattress stuffed with straw,
and every shift and move would call
a watchful parent to the bottom of the ladder,
ear listening for the threat
of unknotting threads.

If our hands were not bound to our sides,
I would salve your palms' pitchfork blisters,
would fold down the stiff collar of your nightshirt,
move past your day in the fields, the barn, the raising
of haystacks and stooks of wheat to those other,
more secret stories.

Though we can whisper
through the dark without reprimand
and memorize each other's faces
by shadow, the sense of touch
must remain in the cedar chest
at the foot of the bed, folded
away with embroidered linens,
crisp cotton sheets, a dark wedding dress
handed down from mother to daughter.

In a place where unbound desire is the snake
in the garden, we could be
simply a boy and a girl leaning into love
and all that's imagined and hoped for,
the substance of things to come;
into that time when just to be this close
is enough, your body next to mine
like steel edging toward flint.

Any stranger passing by this farmhouse in the night
would see the attic's glow and wonder
who lies awake so late behind that window,
who in the darkness left the lantern burning.

Antiromance

No to roses cellophaned
and sprigged with baby's breath.
An even louder no to postcard sunsets
oozing down upon the beach,
two sets of footprints over sand,
a shady picnic pulled from the trunk
of a Mazda Protégé.

Burn the plush bear clutching
his heart-shaped box of truffles.
Ditch the dancefloor feel-up,
sweaty shoulder blades and musk.
Forget the usual progression of
light touch on the small of the back to
streetlamp movie kiss to
won't you come inside?

Any notion of weekend ski lodge getaways
with free champagne and couples massage,
shove into a duffle bag and hurl
off the nearest slope.

Keep that sonnet in your pocket,
along with what the world insists I want—
photo-booth moments,
Ferris wheel flutter in the gut.

Come to me instead with nothing
in your hands, no tricks behind your back,
no shadow up your sleeve. Lay down
the worn-out song, that scratched-up vinyl
stuck in a rut, and I'll hold out
for you a new and naked dance card
with room to write your name,
tell me what you think I need;
I'll show you if you're right.

Secret Sorrows

If the secret sorrows of everyone could be read on their forehead,
how many who now cause envy would suddenly become the objects of pity.

(Italian proverb)

Why scan the racks of glossy magazines
when one can stand in grocery checkout queues
and read the headlines on fellow shoppers,
the real stories behind the coiffed hair,
pressed slacks, unbearably smooth skin?

Why wish for another's brilliance,
when the mathematician's haunted by that one equation,
his mind's blackboard chalking and erasing itself
with numbers, variables, values and signs,
aching for the impossible unknown?

No longer would the life of that suburban lady
have appeal, her secrets bleeding through
like lipstick scrawl above her high-arched brows.

No longer would the millionaire command
such spite, as worry signs its name
and signs its name and signs its name
across the forehead's ledger.

Let what was hidden, the soul seems to say,
rise to the surface and speak.
Drag to the light all the buried texts.

I can read you like a book would be the song
on everybody's lips, or at least on mine
when I crawl into bed beside you.

Though you will not say the words,
your face, its stubborn frail paper burned
by love, gives up its rarest manuscripts.
Everything you've never said, I'll make out,
and let you read the sorrows out of me.
Over one another, we'll write
secrets of a different kind, ones
that night illuminates, and in daylight,
turn the sorry eyes of others back to envy.

The Blue Danube

It was as if we'd stepped inside a television
landscape, the body floating
with its back to the sky, a wide fan
of liquid hair shimmering in blood's
steady push toward shore.

The way any good citizen would
you lay prostrate on the footbridge
and with your driftwood walking stick
pushed at the torso until it dragged
on the silt, the dark head folded down
at the nape like a diver
scanning the shallows.

After our payphone call for help,
we sat on the bridge's edge, our legs dangling,
listened for sirens, and looked
anywhere but down.

From a high apartment window
someone's private orchestra played
On the Beautiful Blue Danube.
The stereo's clear river of swollen
strings streamed through our morning.
The body, a woman's,
moved with the waves.

After the policeman asked us
the same set of questions three times,
after a reporter scribbled
into her notebook a shorthand version
of our finding, after the cameras
had panned the scene and the coroner
zipped shut the long black bag,
we walked the six blocks home,
my hand in yours.

What can we say to each other
on a day like this, at the breakfast
table over coffee and toast, newspaper
spread open to give us tragedies, miracles,
deaths, births, the black and white of life?

How do we hear again the famous melody,
the clear blue river that flows
to the ballroom's edge, shows a young woman
stepping onto the dance floor,
her red evening gown caught in the sway,
her white-gloved hand held out?

Love Poem for a Skeptic

If you were one of the twelve disciples,
no doubt you would be Thomas.

With one eyebrow perpetually raised
in disbelief, arms folded across your chest,
and skeptic heart muttering *yeah, right, as if,*
I'd have to work hard to convince you of my affection,
bring concrete evidence of my love—a lock of hair,
a gold ring, my secret recipe for huckleberry pie.

You're no sucker, not easily duped
by sleight of hand, not even the Saviour's
outstretched over jars of water.

Every time Jesus hushes a storm or heals a leper,
the word *fluke* swims circles in your head.
When the herd of pigs careens off the hillside
into the lake, when the two fish and five loaves
feed a crowd of thousands, even when He
tells a dead girl to wake up and she does,
you can't help but rationalize, think *coincidence.*

Though the lame walk, the deaf hear
and scales fall from the eyes of the blind,
you stand on the margin of every miracle,
still have trouble seeing.

When the other disciples say they've spotted
Jesus alive after the flogging, nailing, death,
you say, show me the proof, let me
shove my hand in His torn-up side.

Now you've come home to me, your kisses
tasting of wine and fire and blood.
After years of parables, desert scorch
and riding out storms in a leaky boat,
you lie in bed beside me and wonder
what's left. In this room of shadows,
truth is the hand you hold in front of your face.
You swear you can see it glowing.

Tame

For weeks you watched the squirrel
dive into our bed of poppies
and come up with chestnuts between its paws.
You stood at the window, witness
to its stuttered movement through leaves,
its constant panic at being found.

To watch from inside was not enough.
You wanted it to eat from your hand,
and sat crouched outside the door
three evenings in a row with a peanut
between forefinger and thumb.

Tonight you have finally lured it
up the brick path and onto the porch,
a foot away from your open hand.
It crouches low and watches you
with its unblinking eyes,
both of you breathing low, unmoving.

The scene could be a framed photograph—
man in doorway, squirrel on edge;
that space between you charged
with the difference between wild and tame.
Like the difference and space that still rises
between us. After a decade of marriage,
it still surfaces. You in some distant corner
of the house, silence laced through you,
and me, waiting alone in that doorway
called resolution or desire.

At the supper table, the chair beside me
stays empty. Your food has not been touched.
Your plate grows cold while you wait
for the animal to give in.

Come, I say to you, holding up
a forkful of mashed potatoes, a piece
of tender meat that falls off the bone.
Whatever will lure you in I'll offer
until all the wildness in you is broken.

Trouble

Aristophanes got it all wrong
about the two hemispheres that split,
meet again in a better life,
love cleaving to its original self.

It's more like the inevitable gravity of trouble,
two halves meeting again and again,
and people whispering,
what do they see in each other anyway?

For example, two friends—call them
Ted & Jean—meet at a holiday dinner party
and start talking about hometowns,
birth order and old scars.

Jean pulls back her sweater cuff to show
the barbed wire's jagged outline
on the inside of her wrist, and Ted unbuttons
his shirtsleeve to reveal a thin white
slit where, as a boy by the fireplace,
his carving tool slipped, and they laugh
a suicide joke, *we must be meant for each other.*

Later in the dark hallway with Kenny G
playing on the stereo he'll dip in close;
Jean will push her lips a little fuller
than usual—she's practised this in the bathroom
mirror—tuck her hair behind her ear,
and the heart-split second splits again.

Love's blood magnet lures its other half.
Her mouth meets his like a homecoming
kiss, a whole new wound they'll wear for life.

Laundry

The intimacy of it implies
the tenuous step toward union,
marriage of dirt and skin and cells.

Undershirts and work pants thrown
with camisoles and stockings.
The piles of our moulting lie
rumpled on the concrete basement floor.

—

Together, we invent creatures.

An octopus of shirt in the dark wet spin.

A many-legged scarecrow
in the drowning chase and slap of pants.

Socks that plaster themselves
against the metal drum,
like birds flattened by glass.

Our offspring are anything but lovely.

—

Down here is where
the deflated arguments go,
laundry inventing its own language.

A knotted pillowcase being a kind of
silent treatment. Reds bleeding
into whites, the obvious hurt.
A sock without its partner, omen
of the empty bed.

But here too is salvation,
where a dripping dress speaks
sadness and regret, and
the unbuttoned shirt offers
forgiveness the way
no mouth can.

—

Underneath all these clothes,
I wish we were strangers
to each other, the kind who
carry their burdens
over the night sidewalks
to haunt the bright laundromats.

This isn't the mess we expected,
the deliberate separation
of dark from light
while the machine drones on
refining its cycle, a continual
submersion and coming
up for air.

Midnight in the Bedroom

It begins with the hunchback and the cantaloupe-sized goitre—
which would you rather have? —a question
sprung on the verge of sleep, that space
where the brain gallops off across the black wilderness
in search of adventure, a stampede of wild mustangs, fire.

And you, turning over in bed, choose the goitre,
say at least you could paint it up like a second head,
wrap a scarf around it, name it, stroke it publicly
in supermarket lineups, for instance.
Give the bored cashiers something to talk about
after a long shift. Goitres, you say, hold mystery,
have cachet in an iodine-rich society.

Like the man in my childhood hometown
standing across from me in the local Co-op produce aisle,
his hand gripping a honeydew or a head of cabbage,
that dark red bulge on the back of his neck.
The guy with the goitre, our family called him,
beige corduroy blazer, thin wisps combed over
to cover his baldness, though who would ever notice
his thinning hair in light of that goitre.

I never learned his name, but he looked like
a Stanley or a Harold, the kind of man who might
spend evenings bent over his stamp collection,
a quiet philatelist listening to Bert Kaempfert
and his orchestra play "Cha Cha Brasilia" or
"Red Roses for a Blue Lady." The music
a Stanley or Harold would love.

Not the music of a Ron or a Ted, Bob Seger
and the Silver Bullet Band, Boston and Steely Dan
cranked up on a back deck party night with Labatt Blue
from the bottle and not the can, hot tub foaming
middle-aged women in two-piece swimsuits
though their bodies have sagged far past that idea, but
Ron or Ted and their yard full of friends don't mind,
still hoot smoky laughter at the moon and hold
cigarette lighters to the suburban sky.

But you are not a Stanley or a Harold, not a Ron or a Ted,
you are a Lance who does not collect stamps or drink beer—
still, if you had to slap your money down in a pub,
what would a Lance ask for—Blue Velvet Martini,
Desert Sunrise, Vermouth Cocktail?

Though you've pulled your pillow over your head,
I can tell you're thinking about how a name determines
one's place in the world, tattoos the soul's signature
onto every first impression.

And if you had to change your name, for example, to Gene
or Merle or Hank, would you wear a cowboy hat, dusty
boots and a twelve-string guitar slung over your shoulder,
would you carry in your heart a soundtrack of wild
hoofbeats and lonesome harmonica, sing
sad goodbyes in the campfire's light?

Would you lie beside me on your midnight bedroll,
one slow hand holding onto my hip, the sound of crickets
stitching the moon to the dark, would you listen to
these questions that spark and flicker, would you
stay awake long enough to answer?

Retrospect

Make it an evening wedding, casual jazz trio
on a moonlight buzz instead of the late morning
string quartet, Pachelbel's swoon
and pizzicato hymns.

Lift the roof off the chapel and let night be our canopy.
Trade the chairs' tacked-on bows
for a floating chandelier of stars.

Rip off the fifty-dollar white satin dress and sew
a linen gown that grows my legs six inches longer,
carves my hips down from their stout peasant heritage;
trade the high white heels for bare feet.

Swap my mother's sad pink dress and face
for her gardening jeans and flannel shirt,
my father's stiff tuxedo for his dark blue GWG's,
pack of Export A tucked in the left breast pocket,
cell phone snapped in the right,
and instead of guilt in both of their ears,
some scrolled word from the future
whispering the goodness of this union.

Instead of my rose bouquet, a paper bag full
of mice set loose in the dark church. Instead
of a man preaching love from the pulpit,
a man juggling fire down the aisle.

Take away those table napkins folded into swans
and reception servers who carry silver trays
to our guests. Strip down their black slacks
and white shirts. Dress them in tights, velvet
frocks and brocade tunics, soft plumed hats
or better yet—just strip them down.

Fold up the white slips of paper inked
with courteous toasts to the bride and groom.
Make everyone sing for their supper
and let their songs be boisterous—
hand-clapping, knee-thumping, foot-stomping,
one part hillbilly jug band,
one part Saturday night house party,
one part reverent choir.

Forget the canapés and petit fours.
Let us eat fat slices of bread hot from the oven,
handfuls of chocolate and bowls of homemade ice cream.

Let's dine at the wide tables set for midnight,
and long past the banquet, find ourselves
together, still hungry for this feast.

Acknowledgements

Some of these poems have appeared, in earlier versions, in *Rhubarb*, *The Malahat Review*, and the anthology *Half in the Sun: An Anthology of Mennonite Writing*. Special thanks to Elsie K. Neufeld and Leonard Neufeldt for their supportive words along the way.

St. Thomas Aquinas' *Summa Theologiae* and Dante's *Inferno* aided in the writing on the seven deadly sins.

"The Banning of Beauty" was inspired by chapter 14 in Philip Yancey's *Rumours of Another World*.

"Afterlife Telegrams" was written after reading Josh Earl's *Washington Times* article on a company that sold delivery of messages into the hereafter.

I'm indebted to my editor, Sharon Caseburg, for her keen eye and generous insights into how a poem might sing more clearly. Thank you also to Turnstone Press for their encouragement of this manuscript.

To my one-of-a-kind family for the stories and pictures that keep coming.

To Donn V. for his constant words of kindness, as well as to the rest of my New Life family for their support.

And finally, to Lance and Amelia for their unflinching honesty and love.